BALLADS AND SONGS

BALLADS & SONGS

BY JOHN DAVIDSON

CONTENTS

TO MY FRIEND

WHAT is between us two, we know :
Shake hands and let the whole world go.

TO MY ENEMY

Unwilling friend, let not your spite abate :
Help me with scorn, and strengthen me with hate.

TO THE NEW WOMEN

FREE to look at fact,
Free to come and go,
Free to think and act,
Now you surely know
The wrongs of womanhead
At last are fairly dead.

Abler than man to vex,
Less able to be good,
Fiercer in your sex,
Wilder in your mood,

Seeking—who knows what?
About the world you grope :
Some of you have thought
Man may be your hope.

Soon again you'll see,
Love and love alone,
As simple as can be,
Can make this life atone.

Be bold and yet be bold,
But be not overbold,
Although the knell be toll'd
Of the tyranny of old.

And meet your splendid doom,
On heaven-scaling wings,
Women, from whose bright womb
The radiant future springs !

TO THE NEW MEN

HEAT the furnace hot;
Smelt the things of thought
Into dross and dew;
Mould the world anew.

More than earth and sea
Is a heart and eye:
Gird yourselves, and try
All the powers that be.

Wicked, cease at once
Troubling; wearied eyes,
Rest you now, while suns
Dawn and moons arise.

'Stablish heaven to-day;

Cleanse the beast-marked brow;

Wipe all tears away :

Do it—do it now !

Love, and hope, and know :

Man—you must adore him :

Let the whole past go :

Think God's thought before Him.

Knowledge is power ?   Above

All else, knowledge is love.

Heat the furnace hot :

Smelt the world-old thought

Into dross and dew;

Mould the earth anew.

A BALLAD IN BLANK VERSE OF THE
MAKING OF A POET

His father's house looked out across a firth
Broad-bosomed like a mere, beside a town
Far in the North, where Time could take his ease,
And Change hold holiday; where Old and New
Weltered upon the border of the world.

'Oh now,' he thought — a youth whose sultry
        eyes,
Bold brow and wanton mouth were not all lust,
But haunted from within and from without
By memories, visions, hopes, divine desires—

'Now may my life beat out upon this shore

A prouder music than the winds and waves

Can compass in their haughtiest moods.   I need

No world more spacious than the region here :

The foam-embroidered firth, a purple path

For argosies that still on pinions speed,

Or fiery-hearted cleave with iron limbs

And bows precipitous the pliant sea;

The sloping shores that fringe the velvet tides

With heavy bullion and with golden lace

Of restless pebble woven and fine spun sand;

The villages that sleep the winter through,

And, wakening with the spring, keep festival

All summer and all autumn: this grey town

That pipes the morning up before the lark

With shrieking steam, and from a hundred stalks

Lacquers the sooty sky; where hammers clang

On iron hulls, and cranes in harbours creak

Rattle and swing, whole cargoes on their necks;

Where men sweat gold that others hoard or spend,

And lurk like vermin in their narrow streets :

This old grey town, this firth, the further strand

Spangled with hamlets, and the wooded steeps,

Whose rocky tops behind each other press,

Fantastically carved like antique helms

High-hung in heaven's cloudy armoury,

Is world enough for me. Here daily dawn

Burns through the smoky east; with fire-shod

    feet

The sun treads heaven, and steps from hill to hill

Downward before the night that still pursues

His crimson wake; here winter plies his craft,

Soldering the years with ice; here spring appears,

Caught in a leafless brake, her garland torn,

Breathless with wonder, and the tears half-dried

Upon her rosy cheek; here summer comes

And wastes his passion like a prodigal
Right royally; and here her golden gains
Free-handed as a harlot autumn spends ;
And here are men to know, women to love.'

His father, woman-hearted, great of soul,
Wilful and proud, save for one little shrine
That held a pinch-beck cross, had closed and
    barred
The many mansions of his intellect.

' My son,' he said—to him, fresh from his firth
And dreams at evening; while his mother sat,
She also with her dingy crucifix
And feeble rushlight, praying for her boy—
' My son, have you decided for the Lord ?
Your mother's heart and mine are exercised
For your salvation.   Will you turn to Christ ?

Now, young and strong, you hanker for the
    world;

But think: the longest life must end at last,

And then come Death and Judgment. Are you fit

To meet your God before the great white throne?

If on the instant Death should summon you,

What doom would the Eternal Judge pronounce—

" Depart from me," or " Sit on My right hand? "

In life it is your privilege to choose,

But after death you have no choice at all.

Die unbelieving, and in endless woe

You must believe throughout eternity.

My son, reject not Christ; he pleads through me;

The Holy Spirit uses my poor words.

How it would fill your mother's heart and mine,

And God's great heart with joy unspeakable,

Were you, a helpless sinner, now to cry,

" Lord I believe: help Thou mine unbelief." '

He clenched his teeth ; his blood, fulfilled of brine,

Of sunset, and his dreams, boomed in his ears.

A vision rose before him; and the sound

Husky and plaintive of his father's voice

Seemed unintelligible and afar.

He saw Apollo on the Dardan beach :

The waves lay still; the winds hung motionless,

And held their breath to hear the rebel god,

Conquered and doomed, with stormy sobbing
    song,

And crashing discords of his golden lyre,

Reluctantly compel the walls of Troy,

Unquarried and unhewn, in supple lines

And massive strength to rise about the town.

A quavering voice shattered his fantasy:

His father's pleading done, his mother cried,

With twitching forehead, scalding tears that broke

The seal of wrinkled eyelids, mortised hands

Where knuckles jutted white: 'Almighty
  God!—

Almighty God!—Oh, save my foolish boy!'

He glanced about the dreary parlour, clenched

His teeth, and once again his blood, fulfilled

Of brine, of sunset, and his dreams, exhaled

A vision. While his parents clutched their hearts,

Expecting his conversion instantly,

And listened if perchance they might o'erhear

The silent heavens burst into applause

Over one lost repentant, he beheld

The Cyprian Aphrodite, all one blush

And glance of passion, from the violet sea

Step inland, fastening as she went her zone.

She reached a gulf that opened in the ground

Deep in a leafless wood and waited there,

Battling the darkness with her wistful eyes.

Then suddenly she blanched and blushed again,

And her divinely pulsing body bowed

With outstretched arms over the yawning earth.

Straightway Adonis, wonderstruck and pale,

Stole from the sepulchre, a moonbeam wraith.

But Aphrodite with a golden cry

That echoed round the world and shook the stars,

Caught him and thawed him in her warm embrace,.

And murmuring kisses bore him to her bower.

Then all the trees were lit with budding flames

Of emerald, and all the meads and leas,

Coverts and shady places, glades and dells,

Odoured and dimly stained with opening flowers,

And loud with love-songs of impassioned birds,

Became the shrine and hostel of the spring.

His wanton face grew sweet and wonderful,

Beholding Aphrodite. But they thought—
His father and his mother, sick with hope—
It was the Holy Ghost's effectual call.
Entranced he rose and glided from the room ;
They, undeceived, like little children sobbed.

Slowly he broke his mother's tender heart,
Until she died in anguish for his sins.
His father then besought him on his knees,
With tears and broken speech and pleading hands,

' My son,' he said, ' you open all the wounds
Daily and nightly of the Lord of Heaven :
You killed your mother, you are killing me :
Is it not sin enough, poor foolish boy ? '

For this was in the North, where Time stands still
And Change holds holiday, where Old and New
Welter upon the border of the world,

And savage faith works woe.

                    'Oh, let me be!'
The dreamer cried, and rushing from the house
He sought the outcast Aphrodite, dull,
Tawdry, unbeautiful, but still divine
Even in the dark streets of a noisome port.

At times he wrote his dreams, rebellious still
That he should be constrained to please himself
As one is eased by roaring on the rack.
Desperate he grew, and wandering by his firth,
Exclaimed against the literature he loved.
'Lies, lies!' he muttered. 'And the noblest, lies!
For no man ever understood a woman,
No woman ever understood a man,
And no man ever understood a man,
No woman ever understood a woman,
And no man ever understood himself,

No woman ever understood herself.

Why should we lie? what penalty is this—

To write, and sing, and think, and speculate,

Hag-ridden by ideas, or 'twixt the shafts

Like broken horses, blinded, bitted, reined,

And whipped about the world by steel-tagged

    creeds!'

Wasted and sad with wantonness, and wan

With fantasy—a furnace seven times hot,

Wherein he tried all things; and wrung with woe

To see his father dying for his sake,

And by the memory of his mother's death,

He yielded tamely and professed himself

Convinced of sin but confident in Christ.

Then to the table of the Lord he went,

Ghastly, with haunted eyes that shone, and limbs

That scarcely bore him, like a heretic
Led to the chamber where tormentors stood
Muffled and silent, earnest to explore,
With cunning flames and cords and engines dire,
The sunken wells of pain, the gloomy gulfs
Obscurely wallowing in the souls of men.

In solemn tones the grey-haired presbyter—
'This is My body which is given for you,
This do in memory of Me.'

               The boy,
Whose blood within him clamoured like a storm,
Uttered a smothered cry and rose, but lo !
The happy triumph on his father's face !
'Why do I not die now ? like husks of corn,
The bread, like vitriol the sip of wine !
I eat and drink damnation to myself
To give my father's troubled spirit peace.'

The stealthy elders creaked about the floor,

Guiding the cup and platter ; looking down,

The children in the gallery smirked and watched

Who took the deepest draught; and ancient
    dames

Crumpled their folded ,handkerchiefs, and
    pressed

With knuckly fingers sprays of southernwood.

Ah ! down no silver beam the Holy Grail

Glided from Heaven, a crimson cup that
    throbbed

As throbs the heart divine; no aching sounds

Of scarce-heard music stole into the aisle,

Like disembodied pulses beating love.

But in the evening by the purple firth

He walked, and saw brown locks upon the brine,

And pale hands beckon him to come away,

Where mermaids, with their harps and golden

  combs,

Sit throned upon the carven antique poops

Of treasure-ships, and soft sea-dirges sing

Over the green-gilt bones of mariners.

He saw vast forms and dreadful draw aside

The flowing crimson curtains of the west

With far-off thundrous rustle, and threaten him

From heaven's porch; beneath his feet the

  earth

Quaked like a flame-sapped bridge that spans the

  wave

Of fiery Phlegethon; and in the wind

An icy voice was borne from some waste place,

Piercing him to the marrow. Night came

  down,

And still he wandered helpless by the firth,

That under clouded skies gleamed black and
    smooth
Like cooling pitch.   But when the moon broke
    out,
And poured athwart the glittering ebony
Torrents of molten silver, hurtling thoughts
Trooped forth disorderly.

                                    ' I'll have no creed,
He said.   ' Though I be weakest of my kind,
I'll have no creed.   Lo ! there is but one creed,
The vulture-phœnix that for ever tears
The soul of man in chains of flesh and blood
Rivetted to the earth; the clime, the time,
Change but its plumage.   Gluttonous bird of
    prey,
More fatal than all famines, plagues and wars,
I wrench you off, although my soul go too !

With bloody claws and dripping beak unfleshed,

Spread out your crackling vans that darken

heaven;

Rabid and curst, fly yelping where you list !

Henceforth I shall be God; for consciousness

Is God : I suffer; I am God : this Self,

That all the universe combines to quell,

Is greater than the universe; and *I*

Am that I am. To think and not be God ?—

It cannot be ! Lo ! I shall spread this news,

And gather to myself a band of Gods—

An army, and go forth against the world,

Conquering and to conquer. Snowy steppes

Of Muscovy, frost-bound Siberian plains,

And scalding sands of Ethiopia,

Where groans oppress the bosom of the wind,

And men in gangs are driven to icy graves,

Or lashed to brutish slavery under suns

Whose sheer beams scorch and flay like burning
  blades,

Shall ring, enfranchised, with divine delight.

At home, where millions mope, in labyrinths

Of hideous streets astray without a clue,

Unfed, unsexed, unsoulled, unhelped, I bring

Life, with the gospel, " Up, quit you like
  Gods ! "

Possessed with this, upon his father's hour

Of new-found happiness he burst, and cried,

' Father, my father, I have news to tell !

I know the word that shall uproot the thrones

Of oldest monarchs, and for ever lay

The doting phantom with the triple crown :

A word dynamic with the power of doom

To blast conventicles and parliaments,

Unsolder federations, crumble states,

And in the fining pot cast continents.

A word that shall a new beginning be,

And out of chaos make the world again.

Behold, my father! we, who heretofore,

Fearful and weak, deep-dyed in Stygian creeds

Against the shafts of pain and woe, have
       walked

The throbbing earth, most vulnerable still

In every pore and nerve: we, trembling things,

Who but an hour ago in frantic dread

Burned palsied women, and with awe beheld

A shaven pate mutter a latin spell

Over a biscuit: we, even we are Gods!

Nothing beneath, about us, or above

Is higher than ourselves. Henceforth degree,

Authority, religion, government,

Employer and employed are obsolete

As penal torture or astrology.

The mighty spirit of the universe,

Conscious in us, shall.' . . .

                         Suddenly aware

Of gaping horror on his father's face,

He paused; and he, the old man, white as death,

With eyes like stars upon the crack of doom,

Rose quaking; and ' The unpardonable sin !—

The unpardonable sin !' he whispered hoarse.

' This was the sin of Lucifer—to make

Himself God's equal.   If I may, my son—

If it be God's will, I shall go to hell

To be beside you.   I shall be there first :

I have not many hours to live.   I thought—

Here as I sat beside your mother's chair—

I—my boy !—I wander somewhat.   Let me—

I'll sit again.—Let me remember now

How happy I have been to-day, my son

A member of the Church of Christ, and I

Beside him at Communion, seeing him

And seeing at the window of heaven the face

Of her who bore him, sweet and glorified.

At home I sit and think that, as he lived

Most absolute in sin, he shall, like Paul

Be as insatiable in doing well.

I think how, when my time comes, I shall go

And tell his mother of his holy life

Of labour for the Lord; and then I see

My boy at last appear before the Throne.

"By what right com'st thou here?" the Judge
    demands.

He hangs his head; but round about him throng

A crowd of souls, who cry "He was our staff;

He led us here." "Sit thou on My right hand,"

The sentence falls; and we, my wife and I,

Awaiting you. . . . There came a devil in

Wearing the likeness of my boy, and said

He was predestined for a reprobate,

A special vessel of the wrath of God.

Holy he was begotten; holy born;

With tearful prayers attended all his life;

Cherished with scrupulous love, and shown the

      path

To heaven by her who ne'er shall see him there;

For out of this there comes but blasphemy

And everlasting Hell. . . . Ah! who are these?

My soul is hustled by a multitude

Of wild-eyed prodigals and wrenched about.

Boy, help me to blaspheme. I cannot face

Without you her that nursed you at her breast.

Let us curse God together and going forth

Plunge headlong in the waves, and be at rest

In Hell for evermore. Some end to this!—

This awful gnawing pain in every part!

Or certainty that this will never end !

This, now, is Hell ! . . .   There was a paltry way

Of fooling God some casuists hit upon.

How went it ? Yes, that God did fore-ordain

And so foreknew that those who should believe

Should enter glory of their own free-will.

Ah ! pink of blasphemies that makes of God

An impotent spectator !   Let us two

Believe in this, and that shall damn us best ! . .

I dare, but cannot; for the Lord of Hosts,

The God of my salvation, is my God :

He, ere the world began, predestined me

To life eternal : to the bitter end

Against my will I persevere, a saint;

And find my will at length the will of God.

What is my son, and what the hopes and fears

Of my dead wife and me before the flame

Of God's pure purpose, His, from whose dread eyes

The earth and heaven fled and found no place !

Beside the crystal river I shall walk

For ever with the Lord. The city of gold,

The jasper walls thereof, the gates of pearl,

The bright foundation-stones of emerald,

Of sapphire, chrysoprase, of every gem,

And the high triumph of unending day

Shall be but wildfire on a summer eve

Beside the exceeding glory of delight,

That shall entrance me with the constant thought

Of how in Hell through all eternity

My son performs the perfect will of God.

Amen. I come, Lord Jesus. If his sin

Be not to death . . . Heaven opens ! ' . . .

      Thus he died;

For this was in the North where Time stands still,

And Change holds holiday; where Old and New

Welter upon the border of the world,

And savage creeds can kill.

               The trembling boy

Knelt down, but dared to think, 'A dreadful

       death!

To die believing in so dull a God,

A useless Hell, a jewel-huckster's Heaven!'

Forthwith it flashed like light across his mind,

'If it be terrible into the hands

Of the living God to fall, how much more dire

To sicken face to face, like our sad age,

Chained to an icy corpse of deity,

Decked though it be and painted and embalmed!'

He took his father's hand and kissed his brow

And, weeping like a woman, watched him long;

Then softly rose and stepped into the night.

He stood beside the house a little space,

Hearing the wind speak low in whispers quaint,

An irresponsible and wandering voice.

But soon he hastened to the water's edge;

For from the shore there came sea-minstrelsy

Of waves that broke upon the hollow beach,

With liquid sound of pearling surges blent,

Cymbals, and muffled drums and dulcimers.

Sparse diamonds in the dead-black dome of night,

A few stars lit the moon-deserted air

And swarthy heaving of the firth obscure.

He, knowing every rock and sandy reach,

All night unfalteringly walked the shore,

While tempest after tempest rose and fell

Within his soul, that like an o'er-wrought sea

Laboured to burst its continent and hang

Some glittering trophy high among the stars.

At last the fugal music of the tide,

With cymbals, muffled drums, and dulcimers,
Into his blood a measured rhythm beat,
And gave his passion scope and way in words.

'How unintelligent, how blind am I,
How vain!' he said.   'A God? a mole, a worm!
An engine frail, of brittle bones conjoined;
With tissue packed; with nerves, transmitting
    force;
And driven by water, thick and coloured red:
That may for some few pence a day be hired
In thousands to be shot at!   Oh, a God,
That lies and steals and murders!   Such a God
Passionate, dissolute, incontinent!
A God that starves in thousands, and ashamed!
Or shameless in the workhouse lurks; that sweats
In mines and foundries!   An enchanted God,
Whose nostrils in a palace breathe perfume,
Whose cracking shoulders hold the palace up,

Whose shoeless feet are rotting in the mire !

A God who said a little while ago,

" I'll have no creed;" and of his Godhood straight

Patched up a creed unwittingly—with which

He went and killed his father.   Subtle lie

That tempts our weakness always ; magical,

And magically changed to suit the time !

" Lo, ye shall be as Gods ! " —the serpent's cry—

Rose up again, " Ye shall be sons of God; "

And now the glosing word is in the air,

" Thou shalt be God by simply taking thought."

And if one could, believing this, convert

A million to be upright, chaste and strong,

Gentle and tolerant, it were but to found

A new religion, bringing new offence,

Setting the child against the father still.

Some thought imprisons us; we set about

To bring the world within the woven spell :

C

Our ruthless creeds that bathe the earth in blood

Are moods by alchemy made dogmas of—

The petrifaction of a metaphor.

No creed for me ! I am a man apart :

A mouthpiece for the creeds of all the world ;

A soulless life that angels may possess

Or demons haunt, wherein the foulest things

May loll at ease beside the loveliest;

A martyr for all mundane moods to tear ;

The slave of every passion ; and the slave

Of heat and cold, of darkness and of light ;

A trembling lyre for every wind to sound.

I am a man set by to overhear

The inner harmony, the very tune

Of Nature's heart; to be a thoroughfare

For all the pageantry of Time ; to catch

The mutterings of the Spirit of the Hour

And make them known ; and of the lowliest

To be the minister, and therefore reign

Prince of the powers of the air, lord of the world

And master of the sea. Within my heart

I'll gather all the universe, and sing

As sweetly as the spheres ; and I shall be

The first of men to understand himself. . .

And lo ! to give me courage comes the dawn,

Crimsoning the smoky east ; and still the sun

With fire-shod feet shall step from hill to hill

Downward before the night ; winter shall ply

His ancient craft, soldering the years with ice ;

And spring appear, caught in a leafless brake,

Breathless with wonder and the tears half-dried

Upon her rosy cheek; summer shall come

And waste his passion like a prodigal

Right royally; and autumn spend her gold

Free-handed as a harlot; men to know,

Women to love are waiting everywhere.'

A BALLAD OF THE EXODUS FROM HOUNDSDITCH

Exodus from Houndsditch. 'That alas ! is impossible as yet, though it is the gist of all writings and wise books, I sometimes think—the goal to be wisely aimed at as the first of all for us. Out of Houndsditch, indeed ! Ah, were we but out, and had our own along with us.'

Carlyle's Journal.

He glowed and flamed with faith in Heaven and
    Hell,
  And travailed for his Church in thought and
    deed ;
They cast him out because he preached too well
    His peremptory creed.

He hid himself among the northern heights ;

He watched the misty torrents, thundering,
fall ;

He watched the shortening days, the lengthening
nights ;

And heard the Lord God call,

'Go back, and noise abroad the wrath to come ;

Ask no man's help ; proclaim me in the
crowd ;

Shall my anointed minister be dumb,

When all my foes are loud ? '

He hastened to the city : in a square

He preached the gospel. 'Fellowmen,' he
cried,

'Jehovah speaks through me ; you shall not
dare

To laugh or turn aside.

'I preach no system nebulous and new ;

   God is, or is not : I have not to sell

Cosmetics for the soul : I offer you

     The choice of Heaven or Hell.

'Heed not bellettrist jargon, nor the rant

   Of wanton art and proud philosophy;

But purge your reason of the subtlest cant,

     And listen now to me.

'These are the grievous times that Paul foretold :

   Men have become self-lovers, moneyers;

Boastful and haughty; scorners of the old;

     Thankless, unholy; worse

'Than apes in lusts unspoken that appal

   Sweet love; of dissolute fantastic mood;

Egoists, artists, scientists; and all

     Haters of what is good.

'Be warned ye sceptics, poets—fools ; refrain

   Who lick the lip and roll the lustful eye ;

Repent, ye rich, that for your pleasures drain

     The heart of labour dry.

'Reformer, bishop, knowledge-monger, quack—

   Kill-Christs !—I am to every mortal sent ;

But chiefly to the wise and good, alack !

     I cry, repent ! repent !

'Ye gentle-hearted, lofty-sprited ones

   Who dream, who hope, who think, and who

     design,

And who perform humane things for men's sons,

     Denying things divine,

'Ye labour nobly, asking no reward ;

   But I pronounce unselfishness a crime,

And tell you that the Great Day of the Lord

     Brags in the womb of time.

'Soon shall the elements with fervent heat
 Melt, and the stars be shed like withered
  leaves;
And ye shall stand before the judgment-seat
 With murderers, liars, thieves.

'Repent! repent! and shun your awful fate!
 Why were your souls to your own bodies lent
But for your own first care! Men, good and great,
 I say, repent! repent!

'And turn to Christ who put his glory by,
 And suffered on the cross that anguish fell;
If you will not believe before you die,
 You shall believe in Hell!'

The chill wind whispered winter; night set in;
 Stars flickered high; and like a tidal wave,
He heard the rolling multitudinous din
 Of life the city lave,

And burst in devious streams and eddying
   wreaths,
  To fill the halls its glowing surges stain,
And hidden nooks wherein it clangs and seethes,
    And spends itself in vain.

 A glittering-eyed and rosy boy that way
   Went past and gravely gazed; a minstrel
   thrummed
His banjo strings; ' Ta-ra-ra-boom-de-ay,'
    A happy harlot hummed.

Then from a shadowy corner of the square,
   A phantom stole and took the preacher's
   hand,
And led him swiftly east to Houndsditch where
    The Aldgate once did stand.

A vapour sank, ill-smelling and unclean,
  Over the orient city; and writhed and curled

Up Houndsditch like a mist in a ravine,

    Of some fantastic world,

Where wild weeds, half-way down the frowning

    bank,

    Flutter like poor apparel stained and sere,

And lamplike flowers with hearts of flame their

    rank

        And baleful blossoms rear.

Nothing he noted of the ceaseless roar

    Of wheels and wearied hoofs and wearied feet,

That sounded hoarse behind 'twixt shore and

    shore

        Of brimming Aldgate Street.

He only heard a murmur gathering fast,

    Of hidden multitudes in wrath and pain;

Anon a visionary pageant passed,

        Through the high-shouldered lane.

But first the bleared and beetling houses
      changed
   To ivied towers and belfries old and gray,
And pointed gables, antic chimneys, ranged
      In ordered disarray.

Then in the midst of Houndsditch one appeared,
   Panting with haste, and bearing heavily
A massive cross; but not as one that feared :
      Rather he seemed to be

With desperate courage flying an event,
   Most woful, unexpected, undesigned,
Born of immaculate heroism, meant
      Wholly to bless mankind.

He sped along a path of cloud and flame,
   That spanned the city, looking ever back
With pity and with horror, till he came
      Where an abyss yawned black.

Straightway he raised the cross high in the air;
　　Its shadow darkened space : into the deep
He threw it : then his terrible despair
　　　　Fell from him, as a sleep

Falls from a young man on a summer morn:
　　Wondering and glad a lowly way he took
By pastures, flowers and fruit, and golden corn,
　　　　And by a murmuring brook:

The while were heard descending from the skies
　　Or out of future times and future lands,
A bruit low and whispers, shadowy cries
　　　　Of joy and clapping hands.

But this scarce-heard applause, so far, so faint,
　　Like happy tears shed in a stormy sea,
Sudden was lost in the deep-voiced complaint,
　　　　The shouts of victory,

Of hope and woe, that with discordant stress

Tempestuously filled the phantom street,

As from its doors there issued forth a press

Of folk with noiseless feet,

That hurried like a torrent through a strait,

And o'er the magic path of flame and cloud—

Arms, voices, of that silent-footed, great

And many-mannered crowd!

Above the street the Holy City hung,

Close as a roof and like a jasper stone

Lit by the Lamp of God; while seraphs sung

And saints adored the Throne.

Beneath, the sewers, flaming suddenly,

Bore down, like offal, souls of men to swell

The reeking cess-pool of humanity,

The hideous nine-orbed Hell.

Templars and warrior-bishops hewed and hacked

Christian and Pagan; kings and priests at feud

Each other smote; king, king—priest, priest
attacked;

Creed, creed—zeal, zeal pursued

With thumbscrews, racks, strappadoes, cord and
stake;

And victims passed: live folk like tired-off toys

Broken and burned—women on fire! Christ's
sake!

And tortured girls and boys!

And there came also gentle counsellors,

And some announced that discord now should
cease;

But every blessing rotted to a curse

Upon the lips of peace.

Then cloth-yard shafts and knightly panoplies

Gave place to ordnance and the musketeer;

And evermore pealed hymns and battle-cries,

And shrieks of pain and fear.

The king o'erthrew the priest; the folk did tame

The king; and, having nobly played the man,

Bowed to the yoke again, while God became

A sleek-haired Anglican.

And still the motley pageant thundering poured

Along the Heaven-roofed and Hell-drained

street—

Priest, trooper, harlot, lawyer, lady, lord,

And all with noiseless feet.

Because the way with living flesh was paved,

With men and women, stifled, broken, bruised,

Whose blood the thresholds of the Churches
  laved,
    And stood in pools, and oozed,

And spirted high like water in a land
  Of mire and moss, at every hoof and foot
Spattering the snowy alb, the jewelled hand
    Of priest and prostitute.

Voiceless and still the human causey lay,
  Until the City of God began to pale,
And Hell grow cold; then from that dolorous way
    Broke forth a feeble wail;

And here and there some sign of life appeared—
  A lifted arm; and faces quick or dead
Surged in the bloody plash; and one upreared
    A ghastly, shrieking head,

That straightway fell, brained by a ruthless hoof:

But the live stones grew stormier evermore,

As dim and dimmer waned the Heavenly roof,

And Hell burned low and lower.

Prone, or half-raised, or upright, desperate blows

By these down-trodden ones were dealt about;

At last the whole live road in wrath arose,

And smote the wanton rout.

Straightway a blood-red fog darkened and shone

And hid the street. . . . Was it the crimson

stain

Of morn alone? Or must the New Day dawn

O'er mountains of the slain?

The mist dissolved : Lo! Nature's comely face!

No Hellish sewer poisoning the air,

No parish Heaven obliterating space,

But earth and sky so fair—

D

Infinite thought, infinite galaxies;

And on a daisied lawn a shining throng

Of noble people sweetly sang : here is

The burden of their song :

'With love and hope we go;

We neither fear nor hate;

We know but what we know;

We have become as Fate.'

Then suddenly the winter fog unclean

Sank o'er the orient city, and writhed and

curled

Up Houndsditch like a mist in a ravine

Of some fantastic world,

Where wild weeds halfway down the frowning

bank

Flutter like poor apparel stained and sere,

And lamplike flowers with hearts of gold their
rank
And baleful blossoms rear.

The preacher, ghastlier than the phantom, cried
'Get thee behind me, Satan!' clutched the
night,
Staggered, ran on, shrieked, laughed, fell down
and died
Of that strange-storied sight.

Few marked his death amid the ceaseless roar
Of wheels and wearied hoofs and wearied teet,
That sounded hoarse behind 'twixt shore and
shore
Of brimming Aldgate Street.

A BALLAD OF A NUN

FROM Eastertide to Eastertide
    For ten long years her patient knees
Engraved the stones—the fittest bride
    Of Christ in all the diocese.

She conquered every earthly lust;
    The abbess loved her more and more;
And, as a mark of perfect trust,
    Made her the keeper of the door.

High on a hill the convent hung,
    Across a duchy looking down,
Where everlasting mountains flung
    Their shadows over tower and town.

The jewels of their lofty snows
  In constellations flashed at night;
Above their crests the moon arose;
  The deep earth shuddered with delight.

Long ere she left her cloudy bed,
  Still dreaming in the orient land,
On many a mountain's happy head
  Dawn lightly laid her rosy hand.

The adventurous sun took Heaven by storm;
  Clouds scattered largesses of rain;
The sounding cities, rich and warm,
  Smouldered and glittered in the plain.

Sometimes it was a wandering wind,
  Sometimes the fragrance of the pine,
Sometimes the thought how others sinned,
  That turned her sweet blood into wine.

Sometimes she heard a serenade
    Complaining sweetly far away :
She said, ' A young man woos a maid ' ;
    And dreamt of love till break of day.

Then would she ply her knotted scourge
    Until she swooned; but evermore
She had the same red sin to purge,
    Poor, passionate keeper of the door !

For still night's starry scroll unfurled,
    And still the day came like a flood :
It was the greatness of the world
    That made her long to use her blood.

In winter-time when Lent drew nigh,
    And hill and plain were wrapped in snow,
She watched beneath the frosty sky
    The nearest city nightly glow.

Like peals of airy bells outworn

   Faint laughter died above her head

In gusts of broken music borne :

   'They keep the Carnival,' she said.

Her hungry heart devoured the town :

   'Heaven save me by a miracle !

Unless God sends an angel down,

   Thither I go though it were Hell.'

She dug her nails deep in her breast,

   Sobbed, shrieked, and straight withdrew the

      bar :

A fledgling flying from the nest,

   A pale moth rushing to a star.

Fillet and veil in strips she tore ;

   Her golden tresses floated wide ;

The ring and bracelet that she wore

   As Christ's betrothed, she cast aside.

Life's dearest meaning I shall probe ;
   Lo ! I shall taste of love at last !
Away ! ' She doffed her outer robe,
   And sent it sailing down the blast.

Her body seemed to warm the wind ;
   With bleeding feet o'er ice she ran :
' I leave the righteous God behind ;
   I go to worship sinful man.'

She reached the sounding city's gate ;
   No question did the warder ask :
He passed her in : ' Welcome, wild mate ! '
   He thought her some fantastic mask.

Half-naked through the town she went ;
   Each footstep left a bloody mark ;
Crowds followed her with looks intent ;
   Her bright eyes made the torches dark.

Alone and watching in the street

There stood a grave youth nobly dressed ;

To him she knelt and kissed his feet ;

Her face her great desire confessed.

Straight to his house the nun he led :

' Strange lady, what would you with me ? '

' Your love, your love, sweet lord,' she said ;

' I bring you my virginity.'

He healed her bosom with a kiss ;

She gave him all her passion's hoard ;

And sobbed and murmured ever, ' This

Is life's great meaning, dear, my lord.

' I care not for my broken vow ;

Though God should come in thunder soon,

I am sister to the mountains now,

And sister to the sun and moon.'

Through all the towns of Belmarie
    She made a progress like a queen.
'She is,' they said, 'whate'er she be,
    The strangest woman ever seen.

'From fairyland she must have come,
    Or else she is a mermaiden.'
Some said she was a ghoul, and some
    A heathen goddess born again.

But soon her fire to ashes burned ;
    Her beauty changed to haggardness ;
Her golden hair to silver turned ;
    The hour came of her last caress.

At midnight from her lonely bed
    She rose, and said, 'I have had my will.'
The old ragged robe she donned, and fled
    Back to the convent on the hill.

Half-naked as she went before,

    She hurried to the city wall,

Unnoticed in the rush and roar

    And splendour of the carnival.

No question did the warder ask :

    Her ragged robe, her shrunken limb,

Her dreadful eyes! 'It is no mask ;

    It is a she-wolf, gaunt and grim ! '

She ran across the icy plain ;

    Her worn blood curdled in the blast ;

Each footstep left a crimson stain ;

    The white-faced moon looked on aghast.

She said between her chattering jaws,

    'Deep peace is mine, I cease to strive;

Oh, comfortable convent laws,

    That bury foolish nuns alive !

' A trowel for my passing-bell,

   A little bed within the wall,

A coverlet of stones ; how well

   I there shall keep the Carnival ! '

Like tired bells chiming in their sleep,

   The wind faint peals of laughter bore;

She stopped her ears and climbed the steep,

   And thundered at the convent door.

It opened straight : she entered in,

   And at the wardress' feet fell prone:

' I come to purge away my sin ;

   Bury me, close me up in stone.'

The wardress raised her tenderly;

   She touched her wet and fast-shut eyes :

' Look, sister; sister, look at me;

   Look; can you see through my disguise ? '

She looked and saw her own sad face,
  And trembled, wondering, 'Who art thou?'
'God sent me down to fill your place:
  I am the Virgin Mary now.'

And with the word, God's mother shone:
  The wanderer whispered, 'Mary, hail!'
The vision helped her to put on
  Bracelet and fillet, ring and veil.

'You are sister to the mountains now,
  And sister to the day and night;
Sister to God.' And on the brow
  She kissed her thrice, and left her sight.

While dreaming in her cloudy bed,
  Far in the crimson orient land,
On many a mountain's happy head
  Dawn lightly laid her rosy hand.

THE VENGEANCE OF THE DUCHESS

THE sun of Austerlitz had dawned and shone
    and set in blood,
When to Illyria Sigismund rode home by fell
    and flood.

'What news, what news, Duke Sigismund?' the
    Duchess Agnes cried.
'Heavy—an avalanche of lead,' Duke Sigismund
    replied.

'Across the astonished land the sun comes con-
    quering from the west—
Napoleon's banners, purpled in the blood of
    Europe's best.'

'Heavy—an avalanche of lead!' she echoed in
    dismay.

'Take heart,' he said. But she, 'Ah me! this
    was our wedding-day

'Five years ago!—Oh! that base churl, and un-
    imagined thief,
That kingdom-breaker! Give me words, or I
    shall die of grief!

'Our wedding-day, and Europe fallen! How
    comes it that earth stands!'
She paced the room across, along, and wrung her
    jewelled hands.

At last a new thought dyed her cheek and set
    her eyes on fire :
'Husband, upon my wedding-day, grant me my
    heart's desire.

'I have a thing to do. Take horse.—You're
    tired, my love? Drink wine—
But come—you must—and ride with me to
    Idria's poisonous mine.'

By circling paths adown the hill they rode, a
    toilsome way;
And came where in a cup-like gap the town of
    Idria lay.

Far in the hideous mine the haughty Duchess
    Agnes found
The thing she sought for buried quick a mile
    beneath the ground :

A ghastly shape of palsied bones across the lamp-
    light dim,
Scarce held together by the chains that bound
    him limb to limb.

While on the earthy slate quicksilver globed
    itself like dew,
He struck the sulphurous cinnabar with feeble
    blows and few.

A clammy sweat welled over him and drenched
    his ragged sash;
Upon his back appeared the curious branch-work
    of the lash.

The Duchess fed her eyes on him unconscious;
    then she said,
'So, Casimir; poor Casimir!' The prisoner
    raised his head,

And ceased his work, but looked not round. She
    whispered to her lord,
'The breathing corpse that swelters here and
    lives this death abhorred,

E

'Dared think of me, the noblest blood and high-
    est heart there is!
Five years ago a youthful god he seemed; now
    is he—this!'

And then aloud: 'Aha! my foster-brother,
    Casimir!
Know then at last that it was I who had you
    buried here.

'You looked to me!—and yet you come of better-
    blooded curs
Than he who tramples on the necks of kings and
    emperors.

'You looked to me, you peasant's son! So on
    my wedding-morn
You here were set, the enduring mark of my for-
    getful scorn.

'From then till now your memory has been a
     bauble thrust
In some disused old cupboard and there left to
     gather dust.

' To-day my suffering soul recalled the vengeance
     I had wrought
On one who hurt my pride by silent look and
     secret thought.

' Under the lash you toil and sweat and know nor
     day nor night,
Rotted with steaming mercury and blanched for
     lack of light.

' In you I came to see what I would make of that
     false knave,
That giant-burglar, Bonaparte, the puddle-
     blooded slave !

'Do you remember Bonaparte who conquered
    Italy?
He is now the master of the world ; while you—
    why, you are he—

'With fortunes cast like Bonaparte's, a match
    perhaps for him—
Who here lie buried quick to please an idle
    woman's whim.'

When she had done he raised his eyes—wide,
    hollow orbs.   She shook
With instant dread, beholding awful meanings
    in his look.

As feeble as a child's his dwindled flesh and
    palsied frame,
But manhood lightened round him from his
    glance of purest flame.

'Agnes,' he sighed ; and that was all he uttered
of rebuke.

He paused, and then melodiously said, though
low, 'You took

'God's way when here you buried me ; nothing
can touch my soul

To discord with the universe. I understand the
whole

'Great wonder of creation : every atom in the
earth

Aches to be man unconsciously, and every living
birth—

'The lowest struggling motion and the fiercest
blood on fire,

The tree, the flower, are pressing towards a
future ever higher,

'To reach that mood august wherein we know
    we suffer pain.

Napoleon! I am greater by this woe and by
    this chain ;

'Because where all blaspheme and die, slaves of
    their agony,

I still am·master of my thought, friend of my
    enemy.

'I reverence the force that was before the world
    began,

And which in me obtained the signal grace to
    be a man.

'Millions of men there are who happy live and
    happy die :

But what of that? I, too, am born a man, I,
    even I!'

He shone on her serenely like a solitary star,

Then turned and toiled in anguish at the
poisonous cinnabar.

The Duchess gnawed her nether lip, but found
no word to say.

'The man is mad,' the Duke declared, and led
his wife away.

Glory to those who conquer Fate and peace to
those who fail !

But who would be the Duchess, who, her victor-
victim pale ?

A BALLAD OF HEAVEN *

HE wrought at one great work for years;
  The world passed by with lofty look:
Sometimes his eyes were dashed with tears;
  Sometimes his lips with laughter shook.

His wife and child went clothed in rags,
  And in a windy garret starved :
He trod his measures on the flags,
  And high on heaven his music carved.

Wistful he grew but never feared;
  For always on the midnight skies
His rich orchestral score appeared
  In stars and zones and galaxies.

* See note at the end of the book.

He thought to copy down his score :

 The moonlight was his lamp : he said,

' Listen, my love ; ' but on the floor

 His wife and child were lying dead.

Her hollow eyes were open wide;

 He deemed she heard with special zest :

Her death's-head infant coldly eyed

 The desert of her shrunken breast.

' Listen, my love : my work is done;

 I tremble as I touch the page

To sign the sentence of the sun

 And crown the great eternal age.

' The slow adagio begins ;

 The winding-sheets are ravelled out

That swathe the minds of men, the sins

 That wrap their rotting souls about.

'The dead are heralded along ;

With silver trumps and golden drums,

And flutes and oboes, keen and strong,

My brave andante singing comes.

'Then like a python's sumptuous dress

The frame of things is cast away,

And out of Time's obscure distress,

The thundering scherzo crashes Day.

'For three great orchestras I hope

My mighty music shall be scored :

On three high hills they shall have scope

With heaven's vault for a sounding-board.

'Sleep well, love ; let your eyelids fall ;

Cover the child ; goodnight, and if . . .

What ? Speak . . . the traitorous end of all !

Both . . . cold and hungry . . . cold and stiff !

' But no, God means us well, I trust :

Dear ones, be happy, hope is nigh :

We are too young to fall to dust,

And too unsatisfied to die.'

He lifted up against his breast

The woman's body stark and wan ;

And to her withered bosom pressed

The little skin-clad skeleton.

'You see you are alive,' he cried.

He rocked them gently to and fro.

' No, no, my love, you have not died ;

Nor you, my little fellow ; no.'

Long in his arms he strained his dead

And crooned an antique lullaby ;

Then laid them on the lowly bed,

And broke down with a doleful cry.

' The love, the hope, the blood, the brain,
 Of her and me, the budding life,
And my great music—all in vain !
 My unscored work, my child, my wife !

' We drop into oblivion,
 And nourish some suburban sod :
My work, this woman, this my son,
 Are now no more : there is no God.

' The world's a dustbin ; we are due,
 And death's cart waits : be life accurst !'
He stumbled down beside the two,
 And clasping them, his great heart burst.

Straightway he stood at heaven's gate,
 Abashed and trembling for his sin :
I trow he had not long to wait,
 For God came out and led him in.

And then there ran a radiant pair,
  Ruddy with haste and eager-eyed
To meet him first upon the stair—
  His wife and child beatified.

They clad him in a robe of light,
  And gave him heavenly food to eat;
Great seraphs praised him to the height,
  Archangels sat about his feet.

God, smiling, took him by the hand,
  And led him to the brink of heaven :
He saw where systems whirling stand,
  Where galaxies like snow are driven.

Dead silence reigned; a shudder ran
  Through space; Time furled his wearied wings;
A slow adagio then began
  Sweetly resolving troubled things.

The dead were heralded along :
As if with drums and trumps of flame,
And flutes and oboes keen and strong,
A brave andante singing came.

Then like a python's sumptuous dress
The frame of things was cast away,
And out of Time's obscure distress
The conquering scherzo thundered Day.

He doubted; but God said 'Even so;
Nothing is lost that's wrought with tears :
The music that you made below
Is now the music of the spheres.'

A BALLAD OF HELL

'A LETTER from my love to-day!
   Oh, unexpected, dear appeal!'
She struck a happy tear away,
   And broke the crimson seal.

'My love, there is no help on earth,
   No help in heaven; the dead-man's bell
Must toll our wedding; our first hearth
   Must be the well-paved floor of hell.'

The colour died from out her face,
   Her eyes like ghostly candles shone;
She cast dread looks about the place,
   Then clenched her teeth and read right on.

'I may not pass the prison door;

    Here must I rot from day to day,

Unless I wed whom I abhor,

    My cousin, Blanche of Valencay.

'At midnight with my dagger keen,

    I'll take my life; it must be so.

Meet me in hell to-night, my queen,

    For weal and woe.'

She laughed although her face was wan,

    She girded on her golden belt,

She took her jewelled ivory fan,

    And at her glowing missal knelt.

Then rose, 'And am I mad?' she said:

    She broke her fan, her belt untied;

With leather girt herself instead,

    And stuck a dagger at her side.

She waited, shuddering in her room,

    Till sleep had fallen on all the house.

She never flinched; she faced her doom :

    They two must sin to keep their vows.

Then out into the night she went,

    And stooping crept by hedge and tree;

Her rose-bush flung a snare of scent,

    And caught a happy memory.

She fell, and lay a minute's space;

    She tore the sward in her distress;

The dewy grass refreshed her face;

    She rose and ran with lifted dress.

She started like a morn-caught ghost

    Once when the moon came out and stood

To watch; the naked road she crossed,

    And dived into the murmuring wood.

F

The branches snatched her streaming cloak;
  A live thing shrieked; she made no stay!
She hurried to the trysting-oak—
  Right well she knew the way.

Without a pause she bared her breast,
  And drove her dagger home and fell,
And lay like one that takes her rest,
  And died and wakened up in hell.

She bathed her spirit in the flame,
  And near the centre took her post;
From all sides to her ears there came,
  The dreary anguish of the lost.

The devil started at her side,
  Comely, and tall, and black as jet.
'I am young Malespina's bride;
  Has he come hither yet?'

' My poppet, welcome to your bed.'

  ' Is Malespina here ? '

' Not he!   To-morrow he must wed

  His cousin Blanche, my dear ! '

' You lie, he died with me to-night.'

  ' Not he ! it was a plot.'   ' You lie.

' My dear, I never lie outright.'

  ' We died at midnight he and I.'

The devil went.   Without a groan

  She, gathered up in one fierce prayer,

Took root in hell's midst all alone,

  And waited for him there.

She dared to make herself at home

  Amidst the wail, the uneasy stir.

The blood-stained flame that filled the dome,

  Scentless and silent, shrouded her.

How long she stayed I cannot tell;
But when she felt his perfidy,
She marched across the floor of hell;
And all the damned stood up to see.

The devil stopped her at the brink :
She shook him off; she cried, ' Away ! '
' My dear, you have gone mad, I think.'
' I was betrayed : I will not stay.'

Across the weltering deep she ran;
A stranger thing was never seen :
The damned stood silent to a man ;
They saw the great gulf set between.

To her it seemed a meadow fair;
And flowers sprang up about her feet ;
She entered heaven; she climbed the stair;
And knelt down at the mercy-seat.

Seraphs and saints with one great voice

    Welcomed that soul that knew not fear ;

Amazed to find it could rejoice,

    Hell raised a hoarse half-human cheer.

LONDON

ATHWART the sky a lowly sigh
  From west to east the sweet wind carried ;
The sun stood still on Primrose Hill ;
  His light in all the city tarried :
The clouds on viewless columns bloomed
Like smouldering lilies unconsumed.

'Oh sweetheart, see ! how shadowy,
  Of some occult magician's rearing,
Or swung in space of heaven's grace
  Dissolving, dimly reappearing,
Afloat upon ethereal tides
St Paul's above the city rides ! '

A rumour broke through the thin smoke

    Enwreathing abbey, tower, and palace,

The parks, the squares, the thoroughfares,

    The million-peopled lanes and alleys,

An ever-muttering prisoned storm,

The heart of London beating warm.

A LOAFER

I HANG about the streets all day,
    At night I hang about ;
I sleep a little when I may,
    But rise betimes the morning's scout ;
For through the year I always hear
    Afar, aloft, a ghostly shout.

My clothes are worn to threads and loops ;
    My skin shows here and there ;
About my face like seaweed droops
    My tangled beard, my tangled hair ;
From cavernous and shaggy brows
    My stony eyes untroubled stare.

I move from eastern wretchedness

   Through Fleet Street and the Strand ;

And as the pleasant people press

   I touch them softly with my hand,

Perhaps to know that still I go

   Alive about a living land.

For, far in front the clouds are riven ;

   I hear the ghostly cry,

As if a still voice fell from heaven

   To where sea-whelmed the drowned folk lie

In sepulchres no tempest stirs

   And only eyeless things pass by.

In Piccadilly spirits pass :

   Oh, eyes and cheeks that glow !

Oh, strength and comeliness ! Alas,

   The lustrous health is earth I know

From shrinking eyes that recognise
  No brother in my rags and woe.

I know no handicraft, no art,
  But I have conquered fate;
For I have chosen the better part,
  And neither hope, nor fear, nor hate.
With placid breath on pain and death,
  My certain alms, alone I wait.

And daily, nightly comes the call,
  The pale unechoing note,
The faint 'Aha!' sent from the wall
  Of heaven, but from no ruddy throat
Of human breed or seraph's seed,
  A phantom voice that cries by rote.

THIRTY BOB A WEEK

I COULDN'T touch a stop and turn a screw,
  And set the blooming world a-work for me,
Like such as cut their teeth—I hope, like you—
  On the handle of a skeleton gold key;
I cut mine on a leek, which I eat it every week :
  I'm a clerk at thirty bob as you can see.

But I don't allow it's luck and all a toss;
  There's no such thing as being starred and
    crossed;
It's just the power of some to be a boss,
  And the bally power of others to be bossed :

I face the music, sir; you bet I ain't a cur;
   Strike me lucky if I don't believe I'm lost !

For like a mole I journey in the dark,
   A-travelling along the underground
From my Pillar'd Halls and broad Suburbean
     Park,
   To come the daily dull official round;
And home again at night with my pipe all alight,
   A-scheming how to count ten bob a pound.

And it's often very cold and very wet,
   And my missis stitches towels for a hunks;
And the Pillar'd Halls is half of it to let—
   Three rooms about the size of travelling
     trunks.
And we cough, my wife and I, to dislocate a sigh,
   When the noisy little kids are in their bunks.

But you never hear her do a growl or whine,

    For she's made of flint and roses, very odd;

And I've got to cut my meaning rather fine,

    Or I'd blubber, for I'm made of greens and

        sod:

So p'r'aps we are in Hell for all that I can tell,

    And lost and damn'd and served up hot to

        God.

I ain't blaspheming, Mr Silver-tongue;

    I'm saying things a bit beyond your art:

Of all the rummy starts you ever sprung,

    Thirty bob a week's the rummiest start!

With your science and your books and your

    the'ries about spooks,

    Did you ever hear of looking in your heart?

I didn't mean your pocket, Mr., no :

    I mean that having children and a wife,

With thirty bob on which to come and go,

   Isn't dancing to the tabor and the fife :

When it doesn't make you drink, by Heaven ! it

     makes you think,

   And notice curious items about life.

I step into my heart and there I meet

   A god-almighty devil singing small,

Who would like to shout and whistle in the street,

   And squelch the passers flat against the wall;

If the whole world was a cake he had the power

     to take,

   He would take it, ask for more, and eat it all.

And I meet a sort of simpleton beside,

   The kind that life is always giving beans;

With thirty bob a week to keep a bride

   He fell in love and married in his teens :

At thirty bob he stuck; but he knows it isn't luck:

He knows the seas are deeper than tureens.

And the god-almighty devil and the fool

That meet me in the High Street on the strike,

When I walk about my heart a-gathering wool,

Are my good and evil angels if you like.

And both of them together in every kind of
weather

Ride me like a double-seated bike.

That's rough a bit and needs its meaning curled.

But I have a high old hot un in my mind—

A most engrugious notion of the world,

That leaves your lightning 'rithmetic behind :

I give it at a glance when I say 'There ain't no
chance,

Nor nothing of the lucky-lottery kind.'

And it's this way that I make it out to be :

No fathers, mothers, countries, climates—none;

Not Adam was responsible for me,

Nor society, nor systems, nary one :

A little sleeping seed, I woke—I did, indeed—

A million years before the blooming sun.

I woke because I thought the time had come ;

Beyond my will there was no other cause ;

And everywhere I found myself at home,

Because I chose to be the thing I was ;

And in whatever shape of mollusc or of ape

I always went according to the laws.

I was the love that chose my mother out ;

I joined two lives and from the union burst ;

My weakness and my strength without a doubt

Are mine alone for ever from the first :

It's just the very same with a difference in the
    name
  As 'Thy will be done.'   You say it if you durst !

They say it daily up and down the land
  As easy as you take a drink, it's true ;
But the difficultest go to understand,
  And the difficultest job a man can do,
Is to come it brave and meek with thirty bob a
    week,
  And feel that that's the proper thing for you.

It's a naked child against a hungry wolf ;
  It's playing bowls upon a splitting wreck ;
It's walking on a string across a gulf
  With millstones fore-and-aft about your neck ;
But the thing is daily done by many and many
    a one;
  And we fall, face forward, fighting, on the deck.
                    G

TO THE STREET PIANO

I

A LABOURER'S WIFE

TUNE—*Ta-ra-ra-boom-de-ay.*

ALL the day I worked and played
When I was a little maid,
Soft and nimble as a mouse,
Living in my father's house.
If I lacked my liberty,
All my thoughts were free as free;
Though my hands were hacked all o'er,
Ah! my heart was never sore.

Oh! once I had my fling!

I romped at ging-go-ring;

I used to dance and sing,

And play at everything.

I never feared the light;

I shrank from no one's sight;

I saw the world was right;

I always slept at night.

What a simpleton was I

To go and marry on the sly!

Now I work and never play :

Three pale children all the day

Fight and whine; and Dick, my man,

Is drunk as often as he can.

Ah! my head and bones are sore,

And my heart is hacked all o'er.

Yet, once I had my fling;

I romped at ging-go-ring;

I used to dance and sing,

And play at everything.

Now I fear the light;

I shrink from every sight;

I see there's nothing right;

I hope to die to-night.

II

AFTER THE END

TUNE—*After the Ball.*

OH sorry meaning! Oh, wistful sound!

Lilted and shouted, whistled and ground,

Still in my brain you will waltz and beat?

Haunt me no longer, tune of the street!

Standing between the quick and the dead,

I buy you off with a word of dread:

What will it matter who danced at the ball,
Or whose heart broke at the end of all?

After the end of all things,
After the years are spent,
After the loom is broken,
After the robe is rent,
Will there be hearts a-beating,
Will friend converse with friend,
Will men and women be lovers,
After the end?

Roses and dew, the stars and the grass,
Kingdoms and homes like fashions must pass,
Seedtime and harvest, sunshine and rain
Cease and be welcomed never again;
But passion and power, courage and truth,
Grace and delight and beauty and youth,

Will they go out like the lights at a ball

With sun, moon and stars, at the end of all?

After the spheral music

Ceases in Heaven's wide room,

After the trump has sounded,

After the crack of doom,

Never will any sweetheart

A loving message send,

Never a blush light the darkness

After the end?

SONG OF A TRAIN

A MONSTER taught
To come to hand
Amain,
As swift as thought
Across the land
The train.

The song it sings
Has an iron sound;
Its iron wings
Like wheels go round.

Crash under bridges,
Flash over ridges,

And vault the downs;
The road is straight—
Nor stile, nor gate;
For milestones—towns!

Voluminous, vanishing, white,
The steam plume trails;
Parallel streaks of light,
The polished rails.

Oh, who can follow?
The little swallow,
The trout of the sky:
But the sun
Is outrun,
And Time passed by.

O'er bosky dens,
By marsh and mead,

Forest and fens

Embodied speed

Is clanked and hurled;

O'er rivers and runnels;

And into the earth

And out again

In death and birth

That know no pain,

For the whole round world

Is a warren of railway tunnels.

Hark! hark! hark!

It screams and cleaves the dark;

And the subterranean night

Is gilt with smoky light.

Then out again apace

It runs its thundering race,

The monster taught

To come to hand

Amain,

That swift as thought

Speeds through the land,

The train.

IN ROMNEY MARSH

As I went down to Dymchurch Wall,
  I heard the South sing o'er the land;
I saw the yellow sunlight fall
  On knolls where Norman churches stand.

And ringing shrilly, taut and lithe,
  Within the wind a core of sound,
The wire from Romney town to Hythe
  Alone its airy journey wound.

A veil of purple vapour flowed
  And trailed its fringe along the Straits;
The upper air like sapphire glowed ;
  And roses filled Heaven's central gates.

Masts in the offing wagged their tops;
   The swinging waves pealed on the shore;
The saffron beach, all diamond drops
   And beads of surge, prolonged the roar.

As I came up from Dymchurch Wall,
   I saw above the Downs' low crest
The crimson brands of sunset fall,
   Flicker and fade from out the west.

Night sank : like flakes of silver fire
   The stars in one great shower came down;
Shrill blew the wind; and shrill the wire
   Rang out from Hythe to Romney town.

The darkly shining salt sea drops
   Streamed as the waves clashed on the shore;
The beach, with all its organ stops
   Pealing again, prolonged the roar.

A CINQUE PORT

Below the down the stranded town,
    What may betide forlornly waits,
With memories of smoky skies,
    When Gallic navies crossed the straits;
When waves with fire and blood grew bright,
And cannon thundered through the night.

With swinging stride the rhythmic tide
    Bore to the harbour barque and sloop;
Across the bar the ship ot war,
    In castled stern and lanterned poop,
Came up with conquests on her lee,
The stately mistress of the sea.

Where argosies have wooed the breeze,

   The simple sheep are feeding now;

And near and far across the bar

   The ploughman whistles at the plough;

Where once the long waves washed the shore,

Larks from their lowly lodgings soar.

Below the down the stranded town

   Hears far away the rollers beat;

About the wall the seabirds call;

   The salt wind murmurs through the street;

Forlorn the sea's forsaken bride,

Awaits the end that shall betide.

SPRING

I

Over hill and dale and fen
 Winds adust and roving strum
Broken music now and then
 Out of hedges, lately dumb,
Snow enshrouded; for again,
 Here and now the Spring is come.

Hungry cold no more shall irk
 Beast or bird on hill or lea;
Rivers in the meadows lurk,
 Whispering on the flowers to be;

Rustics sing about their work;
   Spring is come across the sea.

Pink and emerald buds adorn
   Squares and gardens up and down;
Madge, quite early in the morn,
   Gads about in her new gown;
Daisies in the streets are born;
   Spring is come into the town.

II

CERTAIN, it is not wholly wrong
   To hope that yet the skies may ring
With the due praises that belong
   To April over all the Spring :
If one could only make a song
   The birds would wish to sing.

The beggar starts his pilgrimage;

  And kings their tassel-gentles fly;

The labourer earns a long day's wage;

  The knight, a star of errantry,

With some lost princess for a page

  Strays about Arcady.

Now fetching water in the dusk

  The maidens linger by the wells;

The ploughmen cast their homespun husk,

  And, while old Tuck his chaplet tells,

Themselves in spangled fustian busk,

  And garters girt with bells.

Maid Marian's kirtle, somewhat old,

  A welt of red must now enhance;

Oho! ho ho! in silk and gold

  The gallant hobby horse shall prance;

Sing hey, for Robin Hood the bold;
  Heigh ho, the morris-dance!

Oh foolish fancy, feebly strong!
  To England shall we ever bring
The old mirth back? Yes, yes; nor long
  It shall be till that greater Spring;
And some one yet may make a song
  The birds would like to sing.

III

FOXES peeped from out their dens;
  Day grew pale and olden;
Blackbirds, willow-warblers, wrens
  Staunched their voices golden.

High, oh high, from the opal sky,
  Shouting against the dark,
' Why, why, why must the day go by?'
  Fell a passionate lark.

But the cuckoos beat their brazen gongs,

   Sounding, sounding, so;

And the nightingales poured in starry songs

   A galaxy below.

Slowly tolling, the vesper bell

   Ushered the shadowy night :

Down-a-down in a hawthorn dell

   A boy and a girl and love's delight.

IV

By lichened tree and mossy plinth

   Like living flames of purple fire,

Flooding the wood, the hyacinth

   Uprears its heavy-scented spire.

The redstart shakes its crimson plume,

   Singing alone till evening's fall

Beside the pied and homely bloom

Of wallflower on the crumbling wall.

Now dandelions light the way,

Expecting summer's near approach ;

And, bearing lanterns night and day,

The great marsh-marigolds keep watch.

SUMMER

I

THE poets' May is dead and done
    That warm and soft came shoulder-high
On Leda's twins ; for now the sun
    Scarce breaks the cold and cloudy sky.

But still by fields of grass and corn
    With mantling green like blushes spread,
The milk-maid in the early morn
    Trips with her milkpail on her head.

And still through mists that droop and float,
    Beside the river lingering white,

Dew on his wings and in his note,
  The lark goes singing out of sight.

And still the hawthorn blossoms blow ;
  The belted bee on nectar sups ;
And still the dazzling daisies grow
  Beside the golden buttercups.

II

GLOW-WORM-LIKE the daisies peer ;
  Roses in the thickets fade
Grudging every petal dear ;
  Swinging incense in the shade
The honeysuckle's chandelier
  Twinkles down a shadowy glade.

Now is Nature's restful mood :
  Death-still stands the sombre fir ;

Hardly where the rushes brood
Something crawling makes a stir ;
Hardly in the underwood
Russet pinions softly whirr.

III

ABOVE the shimmering square
Swallows climb the air ;
Like crystal trees the fountain's shower,
A-bloom with many a rainbow flower.

Where the lake is deep
Water-lilies sleep,
Dreaming dreams with open eyes
Enchanted by the dragon-flies—

Azure dragon-flies,
Slivered from the skies,

Chased and burnished, joints and rings,
Elfin magic wands on wings.

Like an army dressed
In diamond mail and crest,
The silent light o'er park and town
In burning phalanxes comes down ;

And lustrous ambuscades
In glittering streets and glades,
Where daisies crowd or people throng,
Keep watch and ward the whole day long.

AUTUMN

I

ALL the waysides now are flowerless;
    Soon the swallows shall be gone,
And the Hamadryads bowerless,
    And the waving harvest done;
But about the river sources
    And the meres,
And the winding watercourses,
    Summer smiles through parting tears.

Wanderers weary, oh, come hither
    Where the green-leaved willows bend,

Where the grasses never wither,
    Or the purling noises end ;
O'er the serried sedge, late blowing,
    Surge and float
Golden flags, their shadows showing
    Deep as in a castle-moat.

Like a ruby of the mosses
    Here the marish pimpernel,
Glowing crimson, still embosses
    Velvet verdure with its bell ;
And the scallop-leaved and splendid
    Silver-weed,
By the maiden breezes tended,
    Wears her flowers of golden brede.

Water-plantain, rosy vagrant,
    Flings his garland on the wave ;

Mint in midstream rises fragrant,

Dressed in green and lilac brave;

And that spies may never harass

In their baths

The shining naiads, purple arras

Of the loosestrife veils the paths.

II

AFTERMATHS of pleasant green

Bind the earth in emerald bands;

Pouring golden in between,

Tides of harvest flood the lands.

Showers of sunlight splash and dapple

The orchard park;

And there the plum hangs and the apple,

Like smouldering gems and lanterns dark.

Let no shallow jester croak!

Fill the barn and brim the bowl!

Here is harvest, starving folk,

Here, with bread for every soul !

Rouse yourselves with happy ditties,

And hither roam,

Forsaking your enchanted cities

To keep the merry harvest-home.

Surely now there needs no sigh !

Bid the piper bring his pipe;

Sound aloud the harvest-cry—

Once again the earth is ripe !

Golden grain in sunlight sleeping,

When winds are laid,

Can dream no dismal dream of weeping

Where broken-hearted women fade.

More than would for all suffice

From the earth's broad bosom pours ;

Yet in cities wolfish eyes

    Haunt the windows and the doors.

Mighty One in Heaven who carvest

    The sparrows' meat,

Bid the hunger and the harvest

    Come together we entreat !

Aftermaths of pleasant green

    Bind the earth in emerald bands;

Pouring golden in between

    Tides of harvest flood the lands.

Let the wain roll home with laughter,

    The piper pipe,

And let the girls come dancing after,

    For once again the earth is ripe.

WINTER

DARKNESS turned on her pillow white;
  A star serenely shone;
Deeply, deeply into the night
  Cut the sword of dawn.

Over the snow the pale east threw
  Abroach where daylight broke,
Crimson stains on the abbey panes
  Above the hamlet smoke.

All night the sad world dreamed;
  The sad world wakes all day,
And casts on the snow a ruddy glow
  From its heart that bleeds for aye.

THE HAPPIEST WAY

WHAT will my father say
  To a poor man's son?
I will think of a way;
  My father must be won.

Love, I know, is strong,
  And breaks the barriers down,
Fighting with sword and song,
  A champion of renown.

But oh, for the lover's art
  That finds the happiest way!
Best to strike at his heart,
  And tell him all to-day?

Or after harvest-home

When the leaves begin to fall,

Hand in hand we'll come,

And he shall tell him all?

But now while sweet birds sing

We can roam in the woods all day,

And swing on the orchard swing :

That is the happiest way.

FOR HESPER JOYCE LE GALLIENNE

WHAT boat is this comes o'er the sea
From islands of eternity?

A little boat, a cradle boat,
The signals at the mast denote;

And in the boat a little life:
Happy husband, happy wife!

IN MEMORIAM
MILDRED LE GALLIENNE

Our songs are sweeter far;

The flowers about our feet

Sweet and more sweet;

And every star

Is starrier,

Because of her.

'A Ballad of Heaven' and 'A Ballad of Hell'
are included here as they will not be reprinted in
'A Random Itinerary' and 'Fleet Street Eclogues,'
and because I should like them to be read along
with 'A Ballad of the Making of a Poet' and
'A Ballad of the Exodus from Houndsditch.'

J. D.

Lightning Source UK Ltd.
Milton Keynes UK
UKOW051804310712

196861UK00001B/11/A